ANIMALS OF THE GRASSLANDS

Giraffes

by Kaitlyn Duling

BELLWETHER MEDIA • MINNEAPOLIS, MN

BLASTOFF!
2
READERS

Note to Librarians, Teachers, and Parents:

Blastoff! Readers are carefully developed by literacy experts and combine standards-based content with developmentally appropriate text.

Level 1 provides the most support through repetition of high-frequency words, light text, predictable sentence patterns, and strong visual support.

Level 2 offers early readers a bit more challenge through simple sentences, increased text load, and less repetition of high-frequency words.

Level 3 advances early-fluent readers toward fluency through increased text and concept load, less reliance on visuals, longer sentences, and more literary language.

Level 4 builds reading stamina by providing more text per page, increased use of punctuation, greater variation in sentence patterns, and increasingly challenging vocabulary.

Level 5 encourages children to move from "learning to read" to "reading to learn" by providing even more text, varied writing styles, and less familiar topics.

Whichever book is right for your reader, Blastoff! Readers are the perfect books to build confidence and encourage a love of reading that will last a lifetime!

This edition first published in 2020 by Bellwether Media, Inc.

No part of this publication may be reproduced in whole or in part without written permission of the publisher. For information regarding permission, write to Bellwether Media, Inc., Attention: Permissions Department, 6012 Blue Circle Drive, Minnetonka, MN 55343.

Library of Congress Cataloging-in-Publication Data

Names: Duling, Kaitlyn, author.
Title: Giraffes / by Kaitlyn Duling.
Description: Minneapolis, MN : Bellwether Media, Inc., [2020] | Series:
    Blastoff! Readers: Animals of the Grasslands | Audience: Age 5-8. |
    Audience: K to Grade 3. | Includes bibliographical references and index.
Identifiers: LCCN 2018058082 (print) | LCCN 2018059270 (ebook) | ISBN
    9781618915986 (ebook) | ISBN 9781644870570 (hardcover : alk. paper)
Subjects: LCSH: Giraffe--Juvenile literature.
Classification: LCC QL737.U56 (ebook) | LCC QL737.U56 D85 2020 (print) | DDC 599.638--dc23
LC record available at https://lccn.loc.gov/2018058082

Text copyright © 2020 by Bellwether Media, Inc. BLASTOFF! READERS and associated logos are trademarks and/or registered trademarks of Bellwether Media, Inc. SCHOLASTIC, CHILDREN'S PRESS, and associated logos are trademarks and/or registered trademarks of Scholastic Inc., 557 Broadway, New York, NY 10012.

Editor: Christina Leaf   Designer: Laura Sowers

Printed in the United States of America, North Mankato, MN.

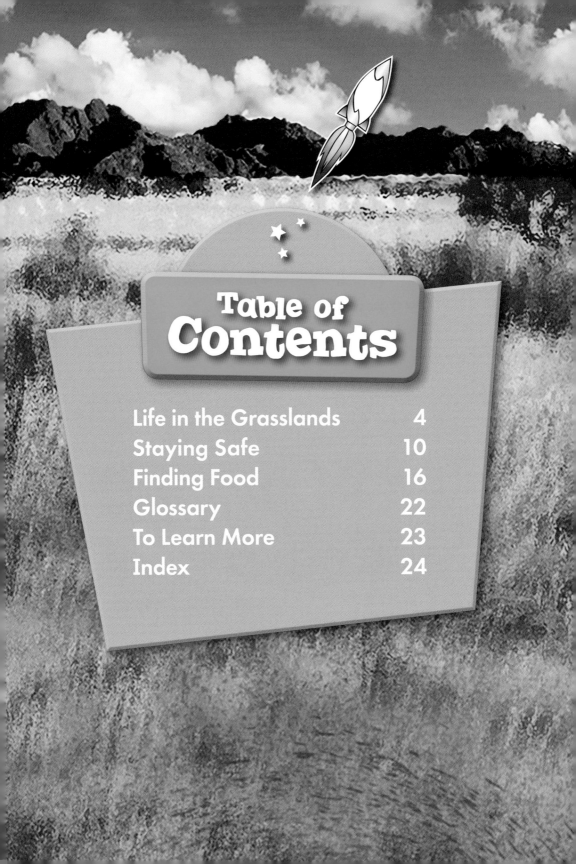

Table of Contents

Life in the Grasslands

Giraffes are the tallest
animals in the world!
They live on the flat
grasslands of Africa.

They are **adapted** to the hot, dry **savanna**.

Giraffe Range

range = ☐

Giraffes blend in with their grassy **biome**. Dark brown spots **camouflage** them from **predators**.

The spots also let off heat
to help keep giraffes cool.

Giraffe tongues have also adapted to the grasslands. The dark color **protects** them from the sun.

Special Adaptations

long neck

dark tongue

dark spots

long legs

Saliva protects their tongues, too. It coats sharp thorns found in their food.

Staying Safe

Tall giraffes stand out on the grasslands. They must watch out for predators.

Long necks help them spot hyenas and lions in the grass.

herd

To stay safe, giraffes do not sleep much. Some only need 30 minutes each day!

One giraffe is the lookout while the **herd** sleeps or eats.

Giraffes run fast
from predators on
their long legs.

If a predator gets too
close, giraffes can kick.

Finding Food

The savanna is hot and dry, but giraffes can go days without water.

Giraffe Diet

acacia trees

wild apricot trees

mimosa leaves

They get most of their water from food. They also sip on morning **dew**.

Giraffe necks can be up to 6 feet (1.8 meters) long! They help giraffes eat food other animals cannot reach.

Giraffes can pluck leaves from tall acacia trees.

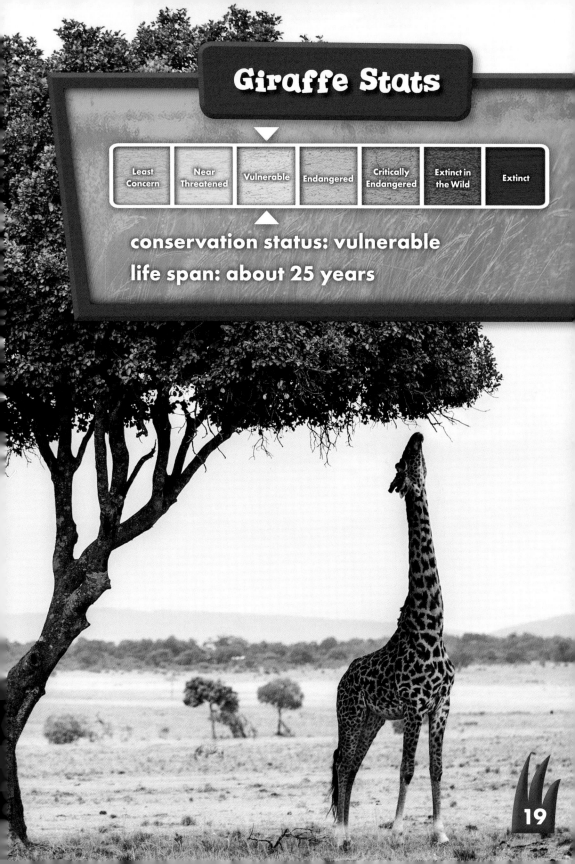

Giraffe Stats

Least Concern	Near Threatened	Vulnerable	Endangered	Critically Endangered	Extinct in the Wild	Extinct

conservation status: vulnerable

life span: about 25 years

Long tongues help giraffes
grab leaves.

The grasslands give giraffes plenty of room to roam and eat!

Glossary

adapted—well suited due to changes over a long period of time

biome—a large area with certain plants, animals, and weather

camouflage—to use colors and patterns to help an animal hide in its surroundings

dew—tiny drops of water that form on plants at night

herd—a group of giraffes that live and travel together

predators—animals that hunt other animals for food

protects—keeps safe

saliva—watery liquid in the mouth that helps break down food

savanna—a flat grassland with few trees

To Learn More

AT THE LIBRARY

Bell, Samantha S. *Meet a Baby Giraffe*. Minneapolis, Minn.: Lerner Publications Company, 2016.

Dussling, Jennifer. *Giraffes*. New York, N.Y.: Penguin Young Readers, 2016.

Walendorf, Kurt. *How Tall Is a Giraffe?*. Mankato, Minn.: Child's World, 2017.

ON THE WEB

FACTSURFER

Factsurfer.com gives you a safe, fun way to find more information.

1. Go to www.factsurfer.com.

2. Enter "giraffes" into the search box and click 🔍.

3. Select your book cover to see a list of related web sites.

Index

The images in this book are reproduced through the courtesy of: E. O, front cover; Volodymyr Burdiak, pp. 4-5; Mayabuns, p. 6; Cathy Withers-Clarke, p. 7; RuthChoi, p. 8; Big Foot Productions, p. 9 (left); Kit Korzun, p. 9 (right); Gudkov Andrey, p. 10; Brian S, p. 11; Ondrej Prosicky, pp. 12-13; Richard Seely, p. 14; Biosphoto/ Alamy Stock Photo, pp. 14-15; ilovezion, pp. 16-17; Jen Watson, p. 17 (left), 22; eelnosiva, p. 17 (right); Rotational, p. 17 (bottom); 3plusX, p. 18; BlueOrange Studio, pp. 18-19; aragami12345s, pp. 20-21; ChrisVanLennepPhoto, p. 21.